KIDDIE CANVAS By KC

Animal Affirmations

Created with love by:
Elodie Romulus

Narrator/Editor:
Koraun Campblin

Kiddie Canvas Books

Dedicated to all kids everywhere — may you always know you are strong, kind, and enough!

How To Use This Book

Welcome to Kiddie Canvas By KC: Animal Affirmations!
This book is designed to be a 3-in-1 experience — making screen-free time fun, interactive, and uplifting.
Here's how to use it:

- Read the affirmation on each page out loud — let the words build confidence and positivity.
- Guess and write the name of the animal you see — make it a fun challenge with friends or family.
- Color the page — bringing the affirmation and animal to life with your creativity.

Each activity is simple but powerful: reading, thinking, and creating all at once. By the time you finish, you'll have a book full of color and confidence!

I AM BRAVE LIKE A:

____

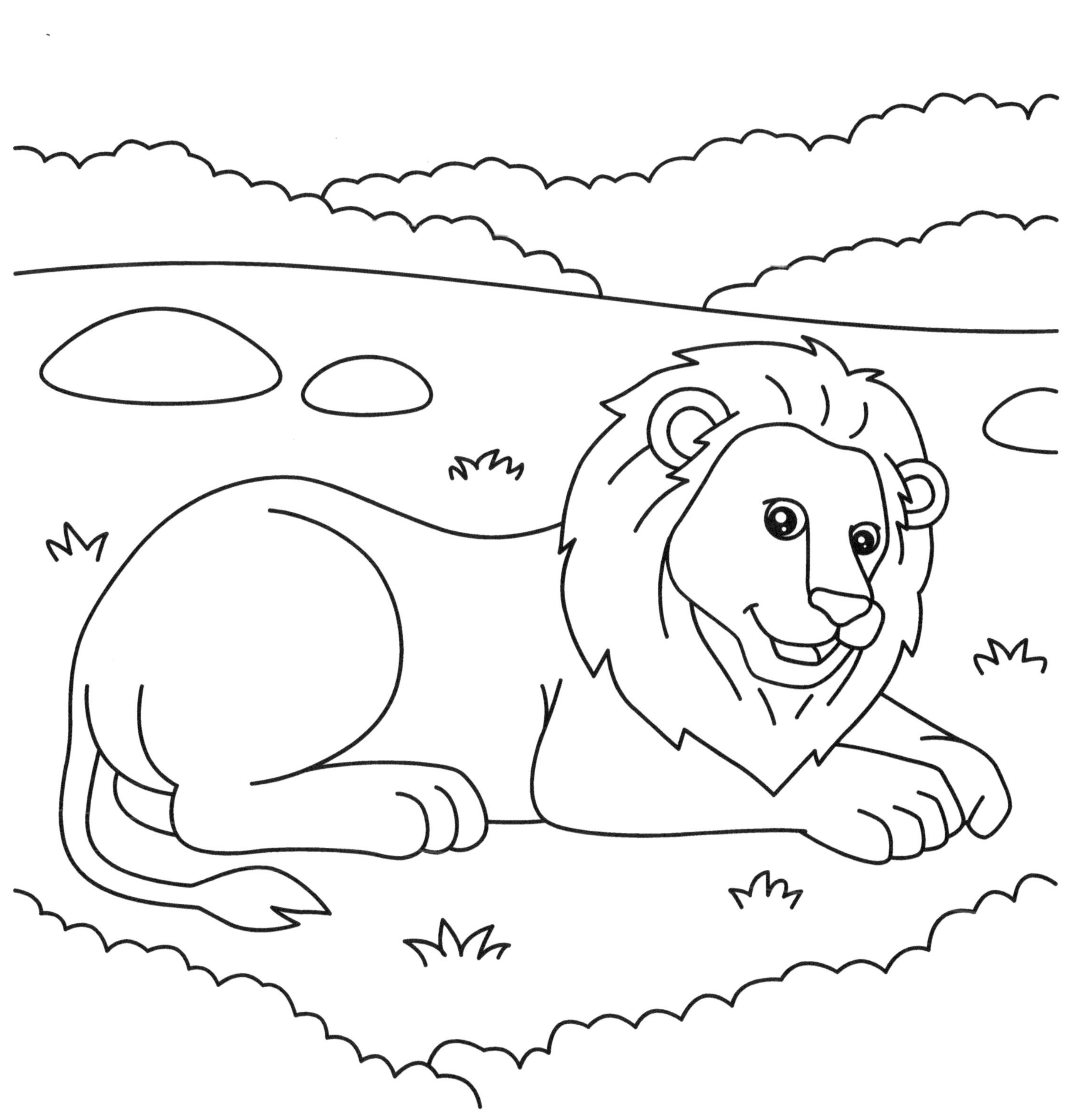

I STAND TALL LIKE A:

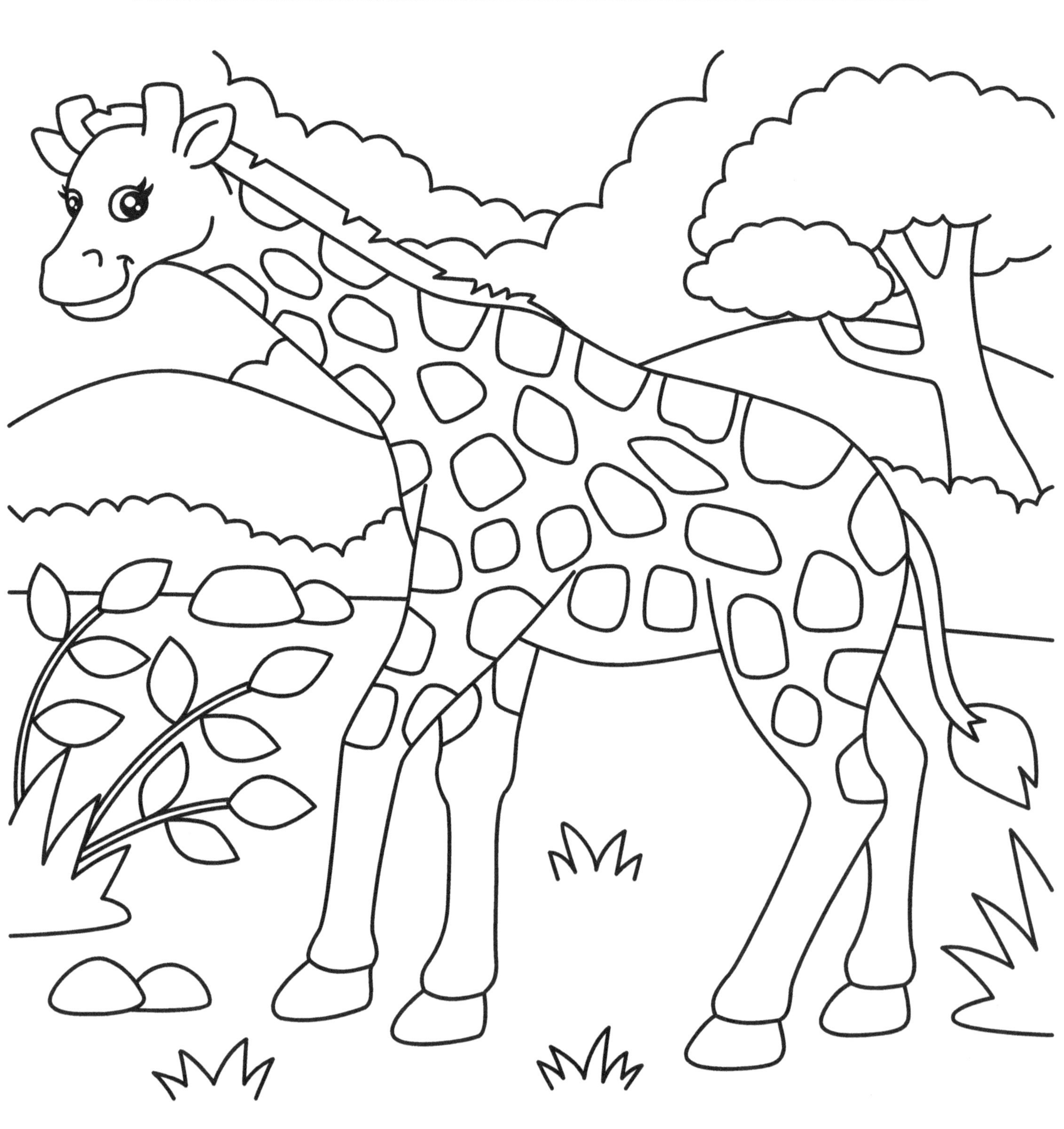

I SHINE BRIGHT LIKE A:

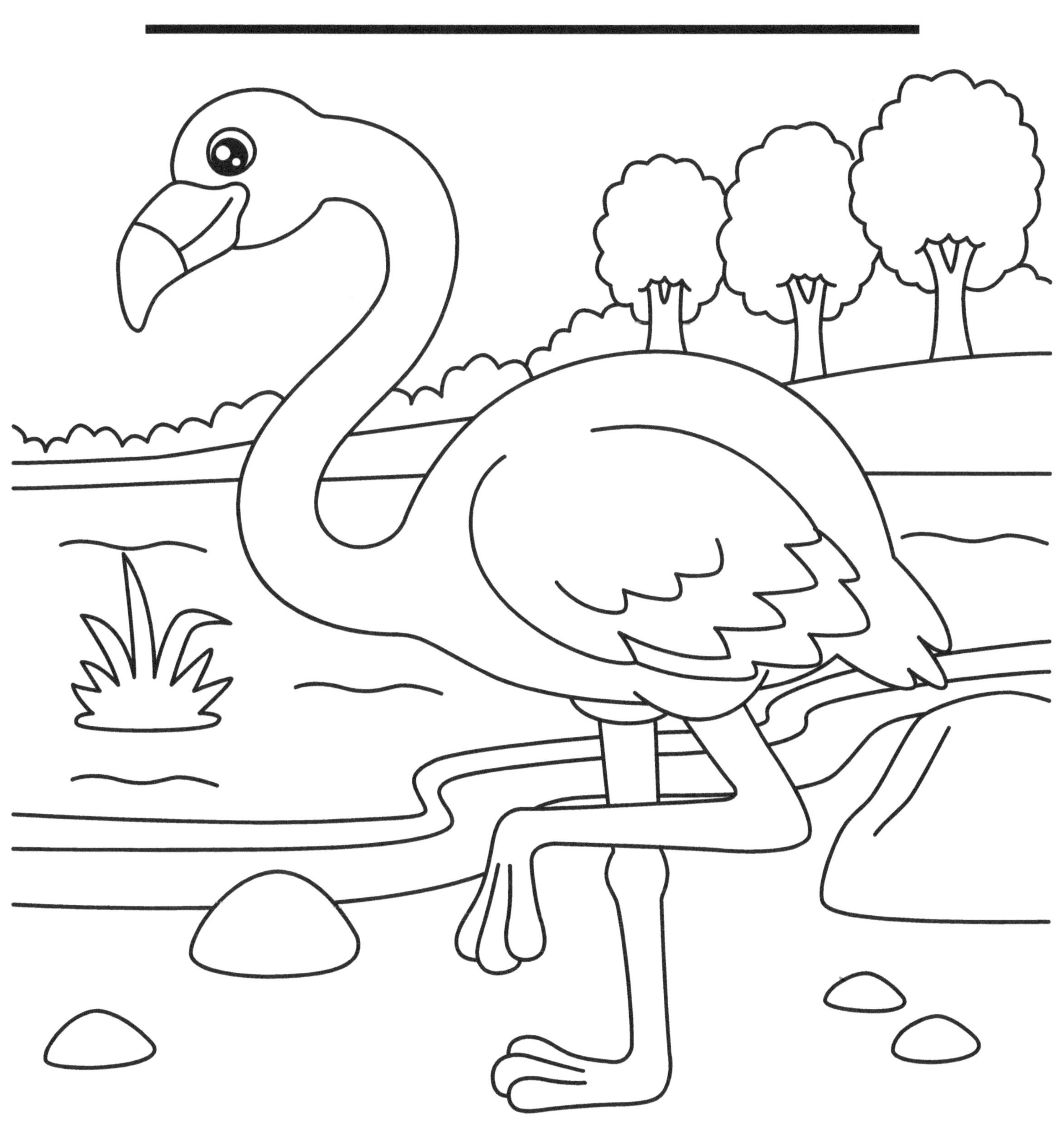

I AM SMART LIKE AN:

____

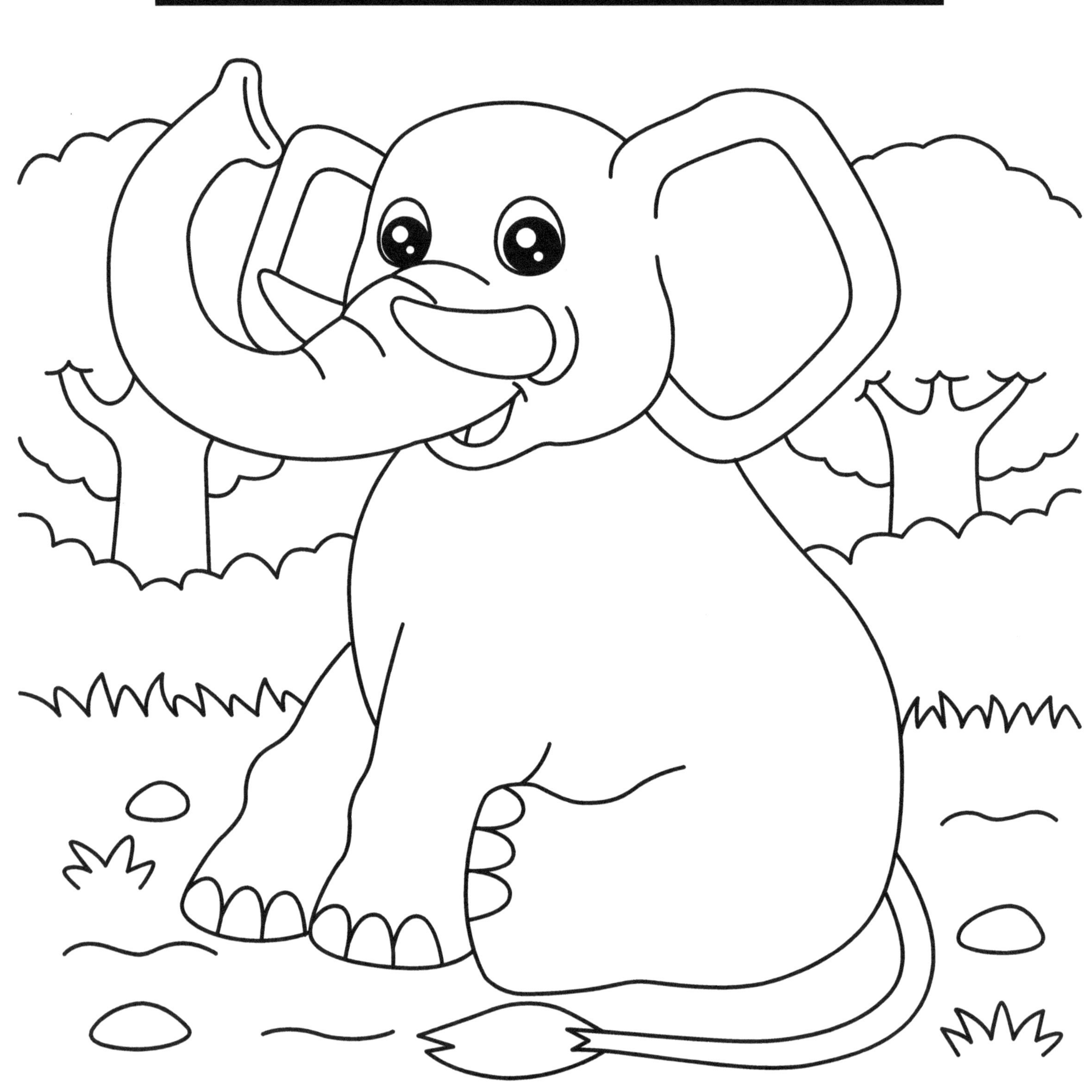

I RUN FREE LIKE A:

____

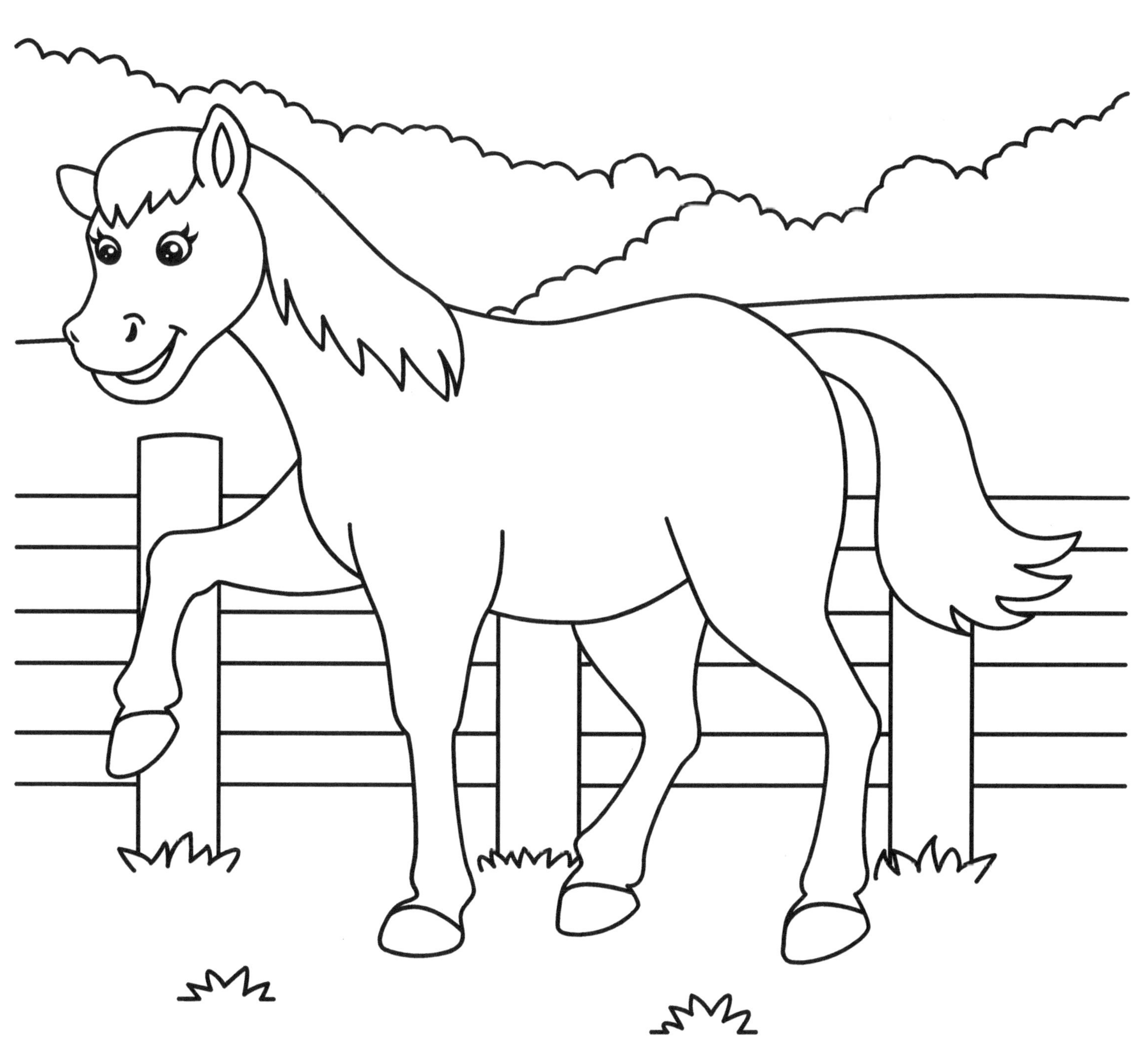

I AM FAST LIKE A:

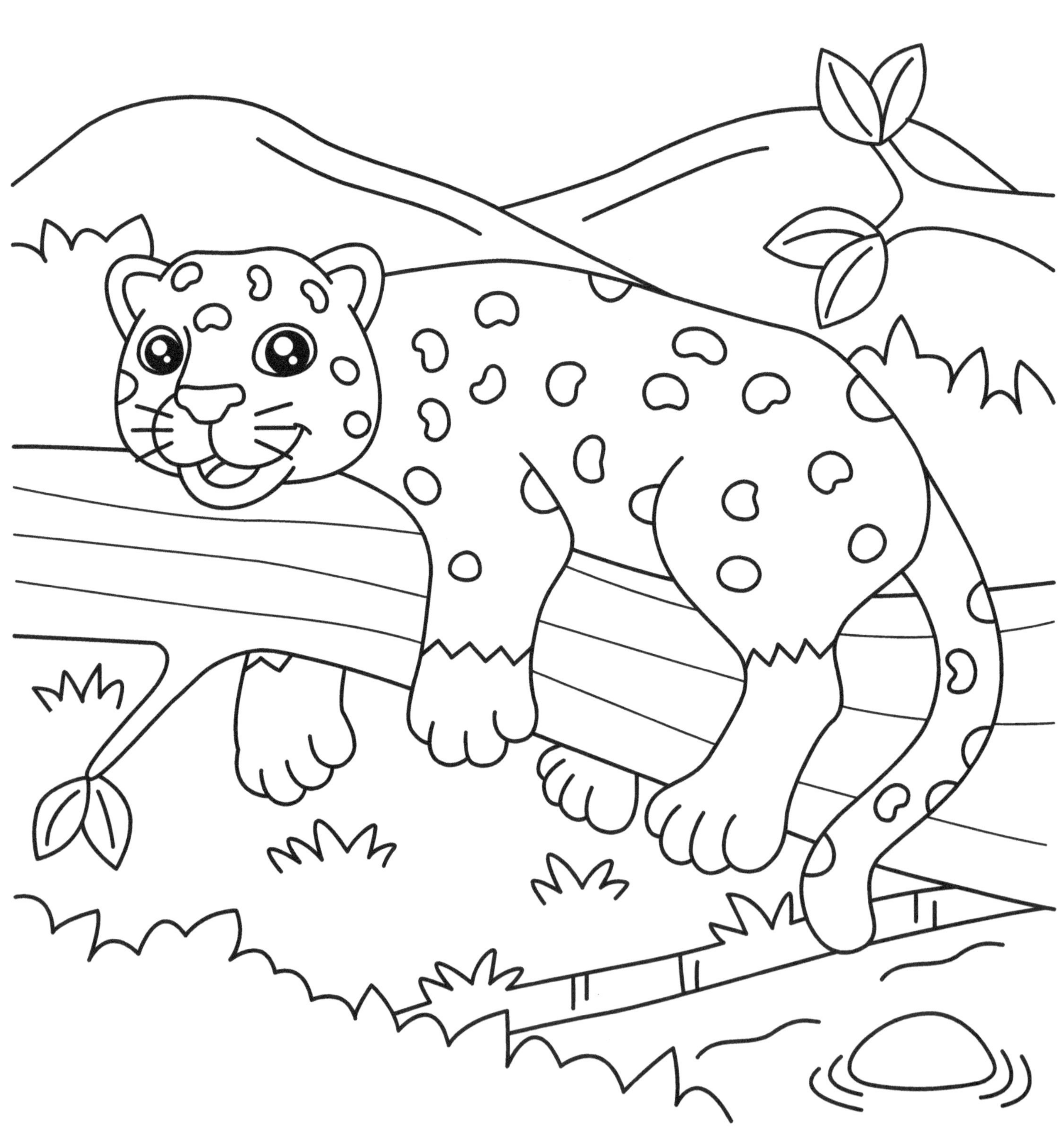

I LEAP HIGH LIKE A:

____

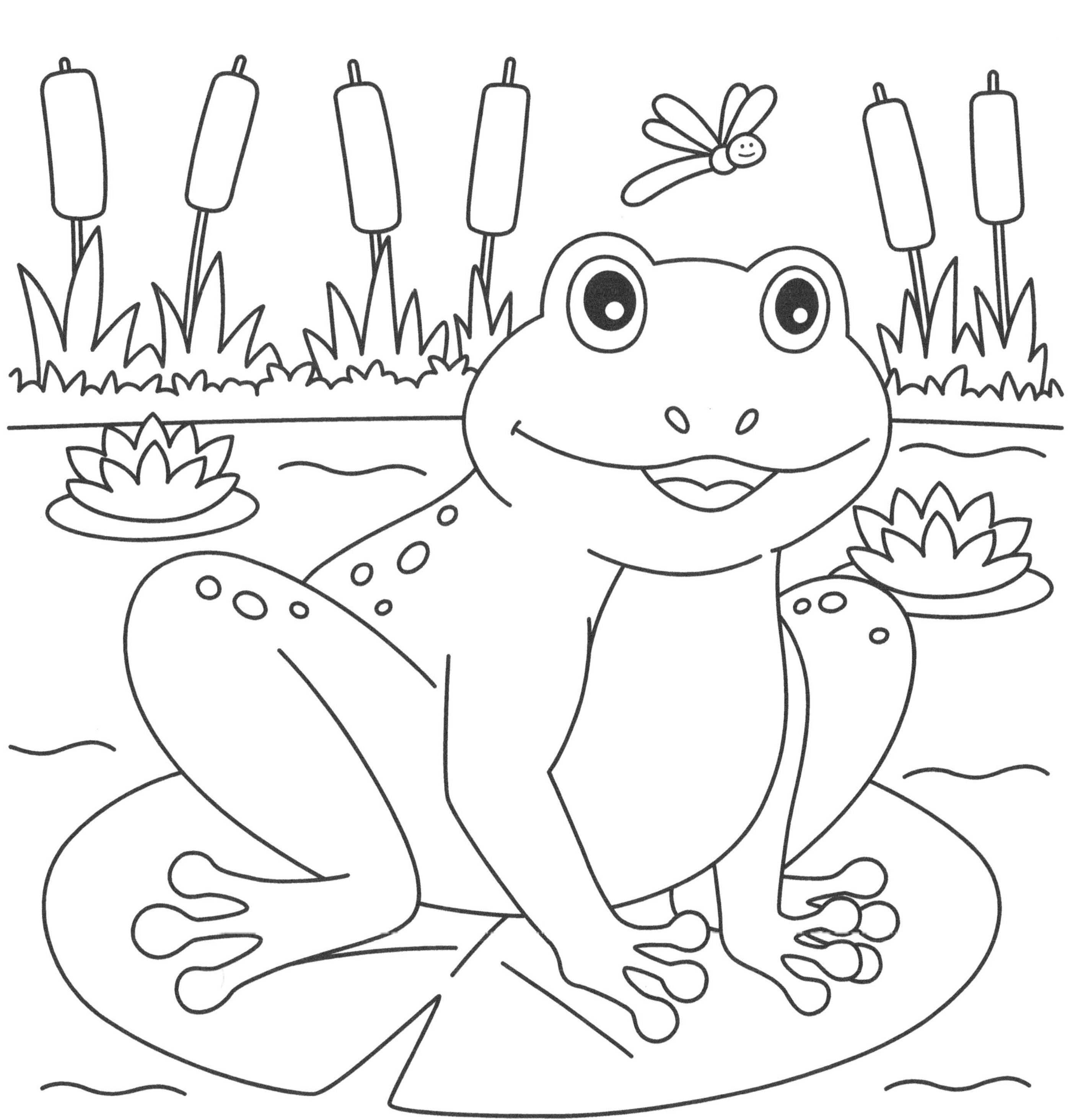

I AM FEARLESS LIKE AN:

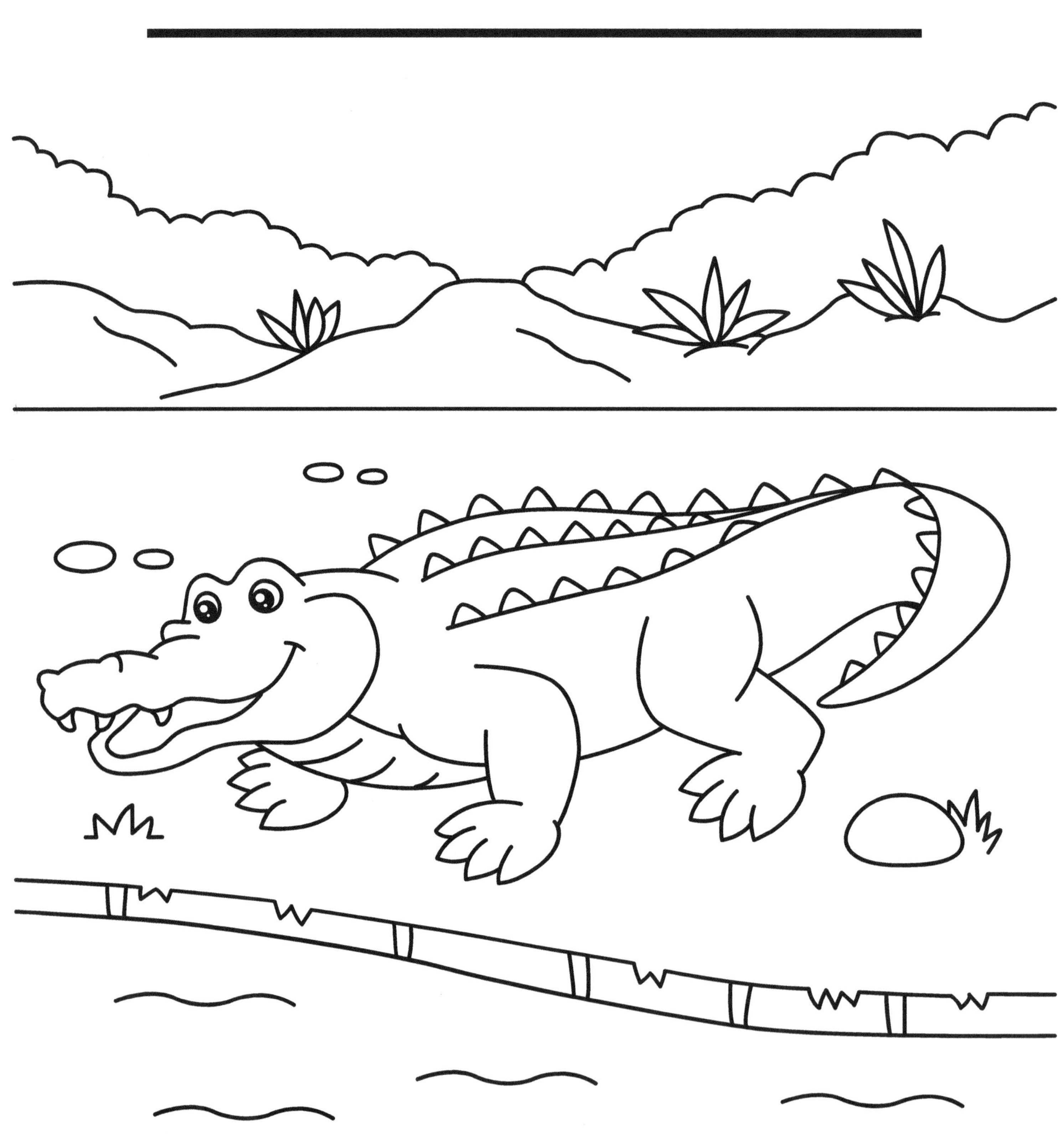

I AM LOYAL LIKE A:

____

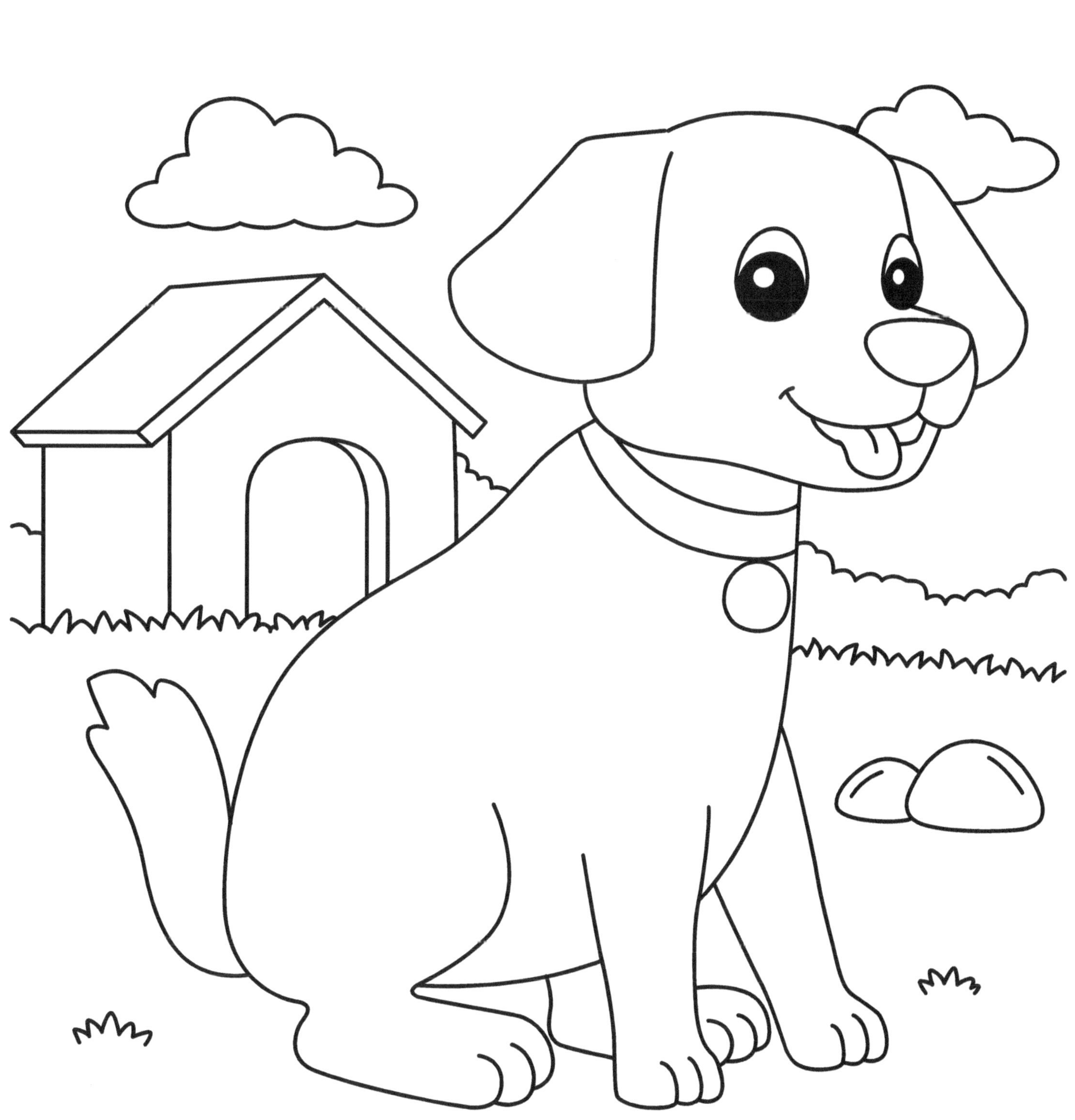

I AM UNIQUE LIKE A:

____

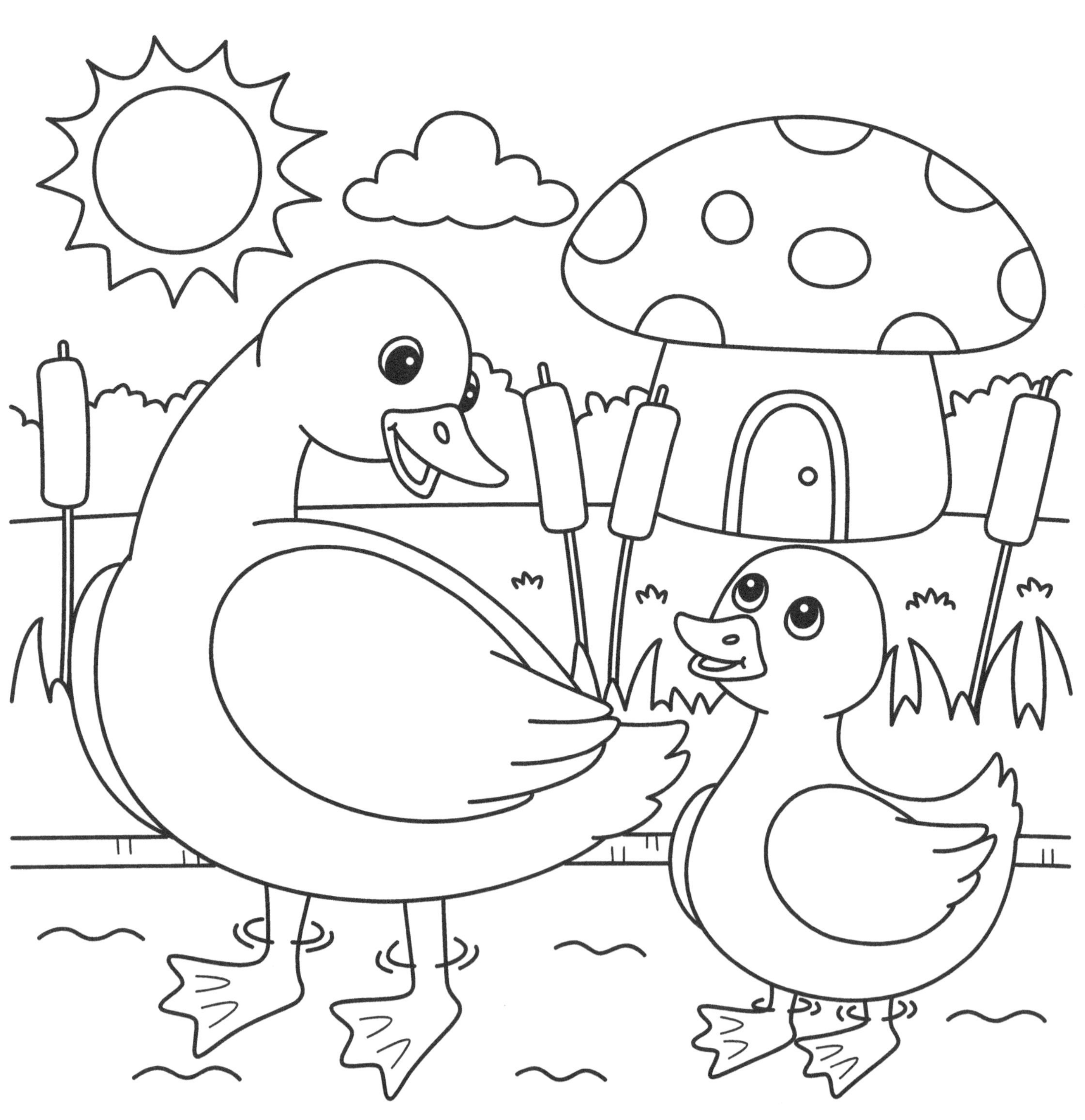

I FLY HIGH LIKE A:

____

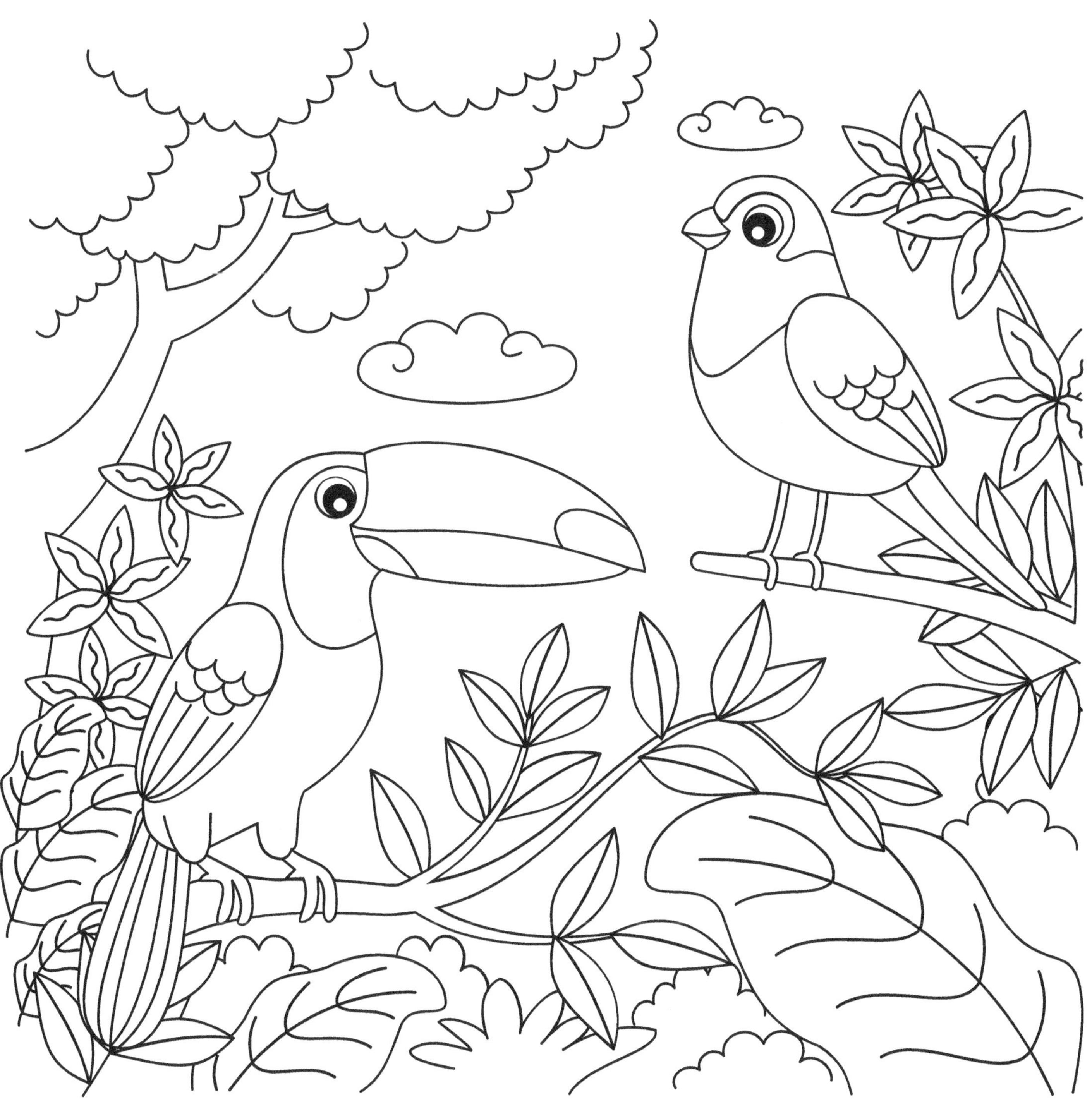

I AM CONFIDENT LIKE A:

____

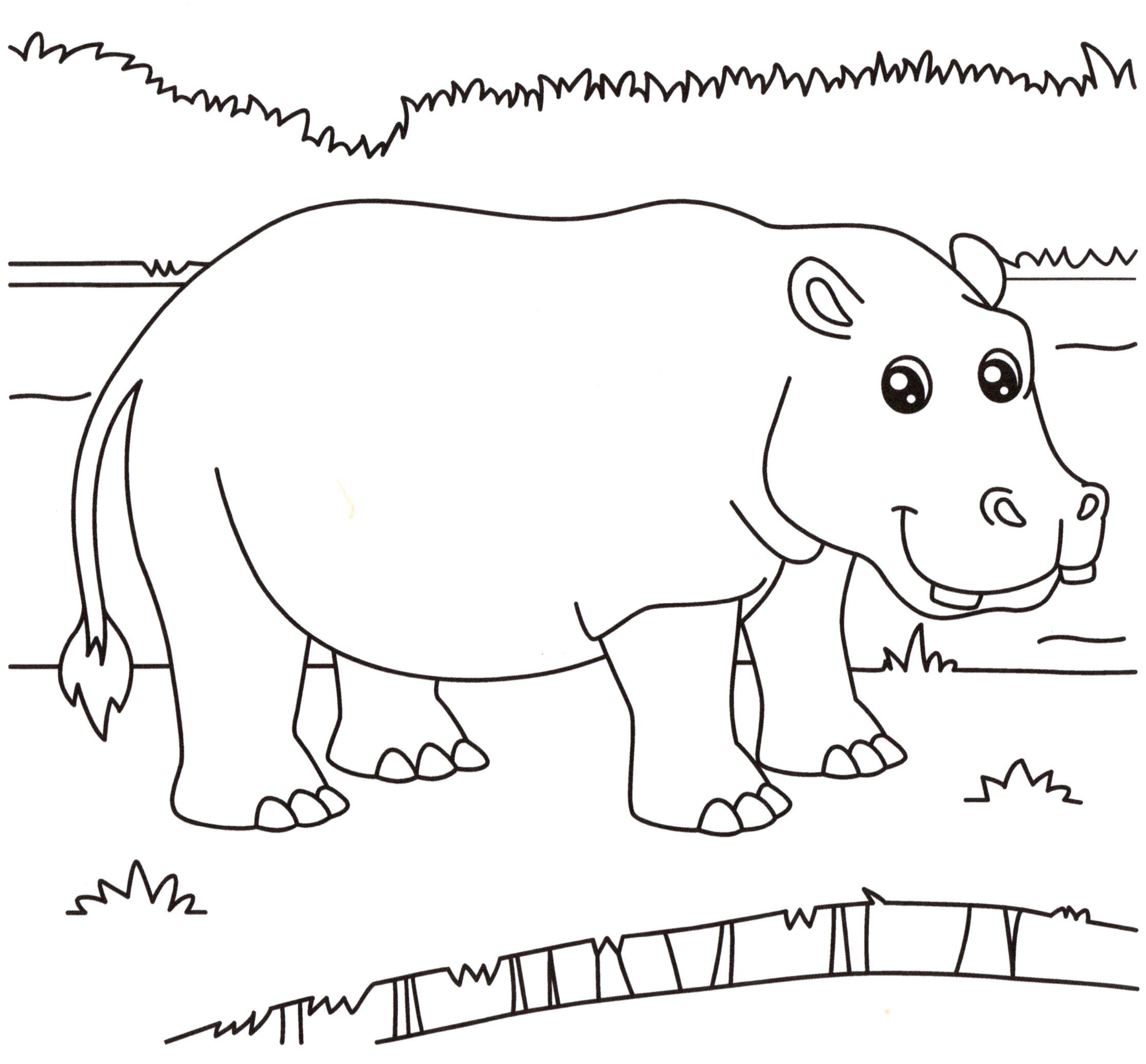

I AM LOVING LIKE A:

____

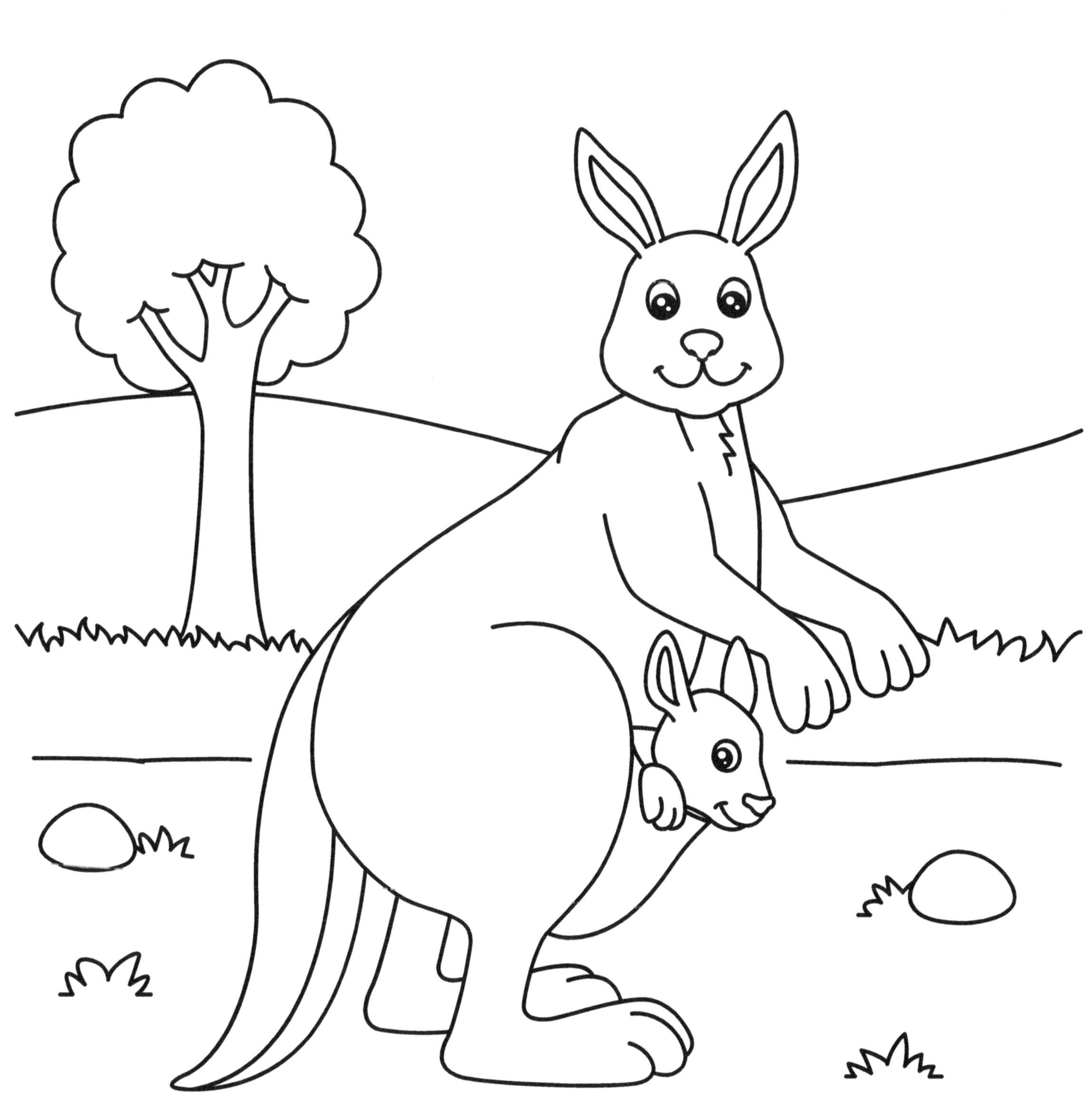

I AM AWESOME LIKE A:

____

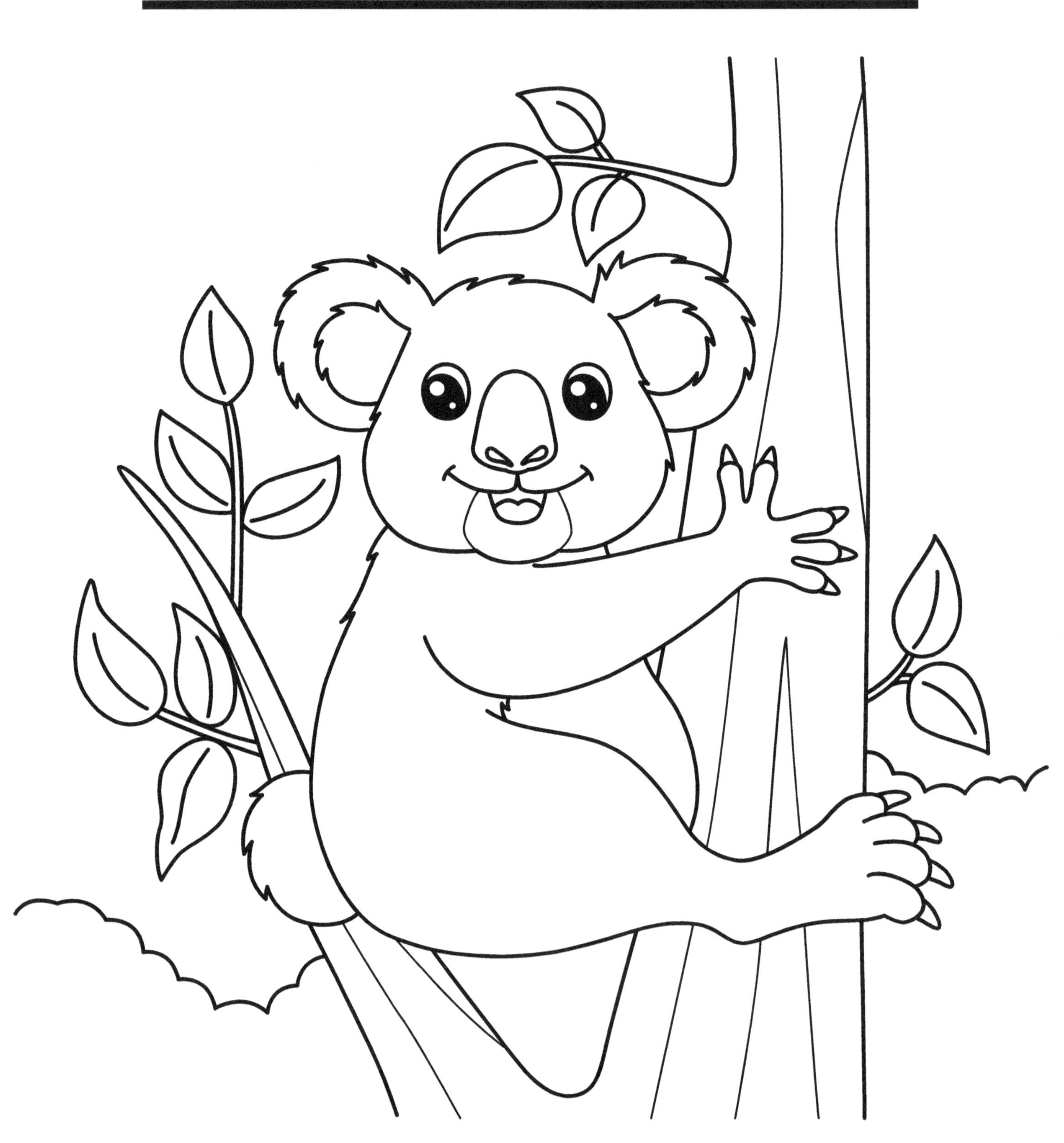

I AM FUNNY LIKE A:

____

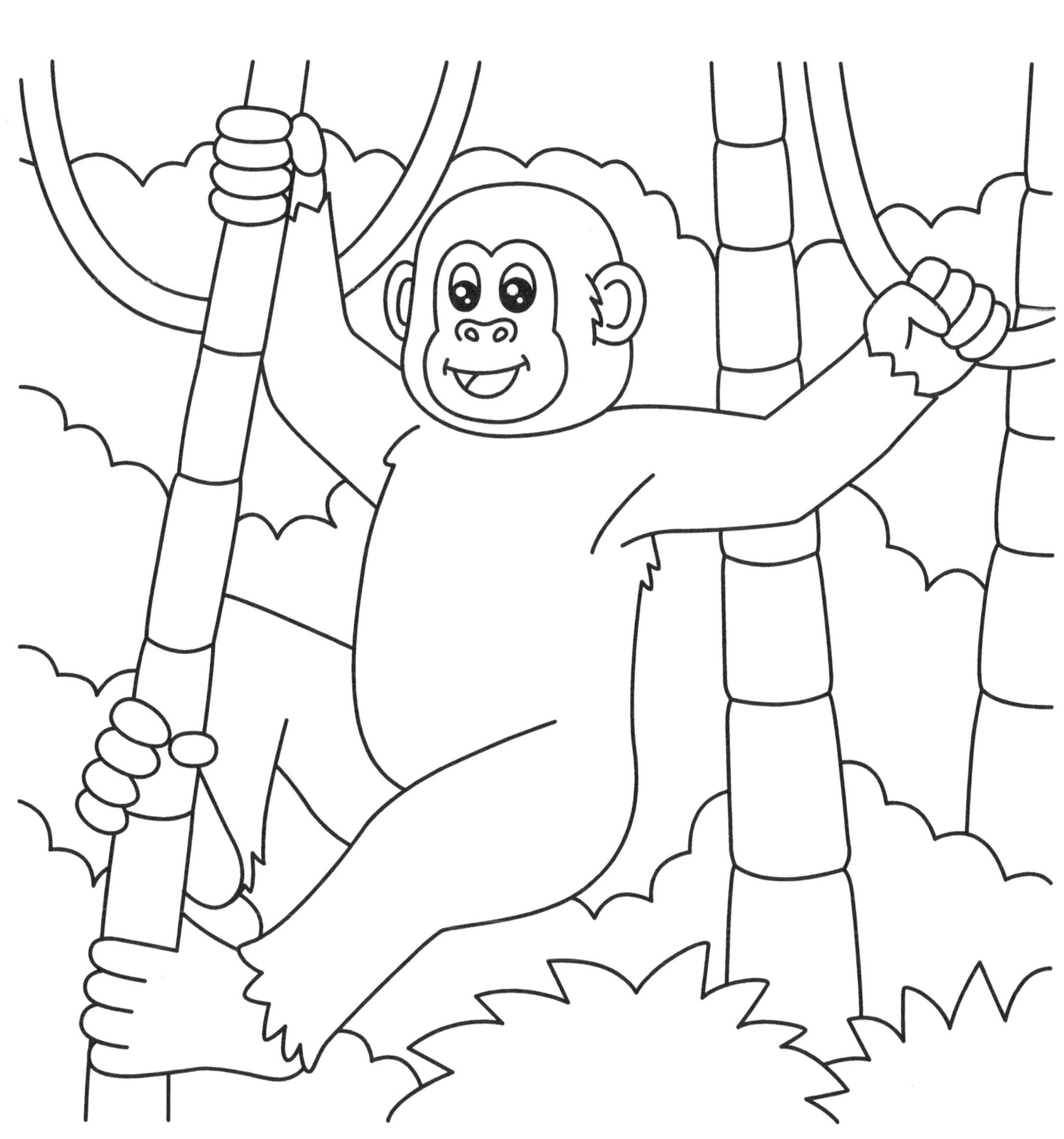

I AM GENTLE LIKE A:

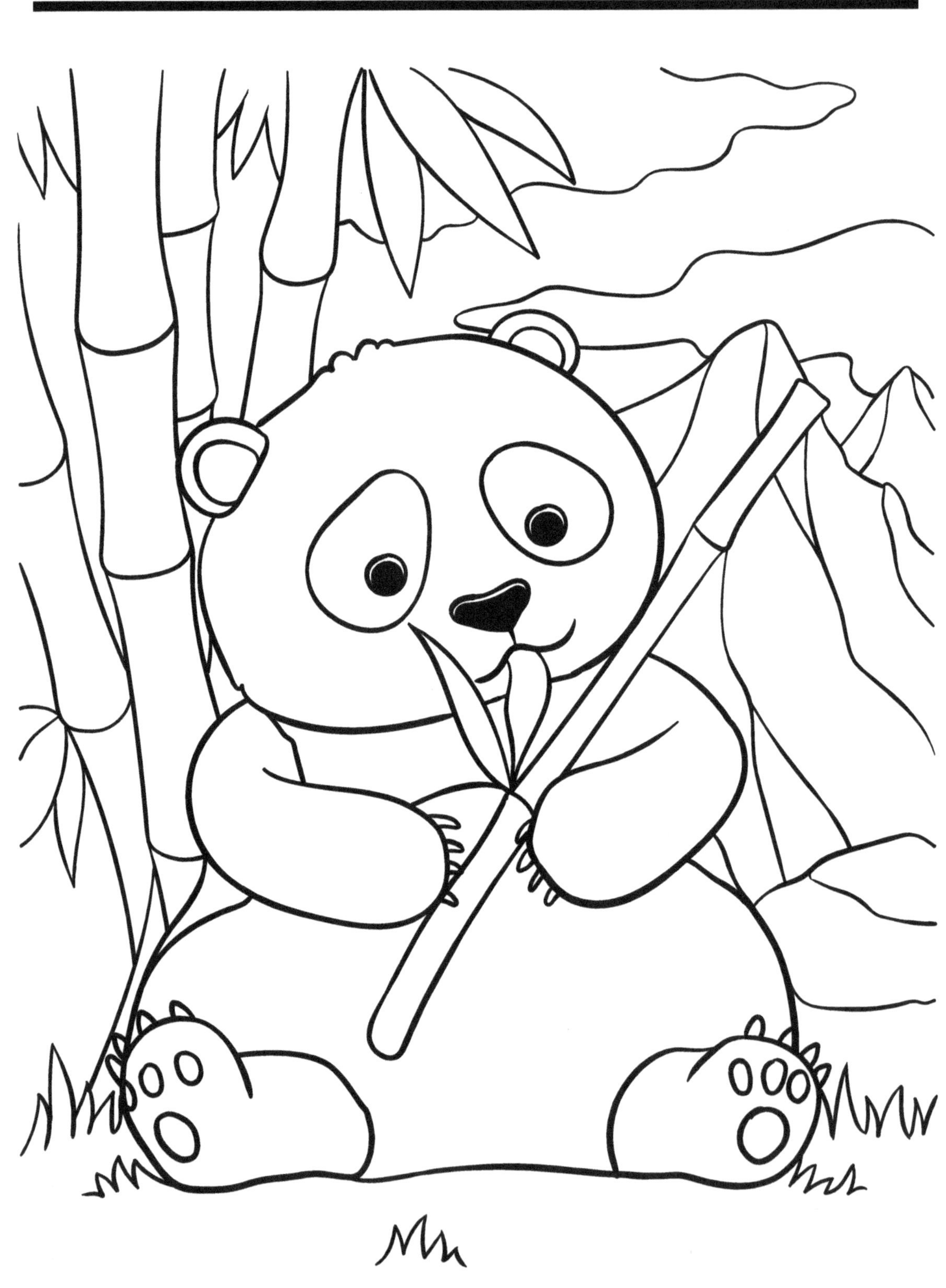

I AM BOLD LIKE A:

____

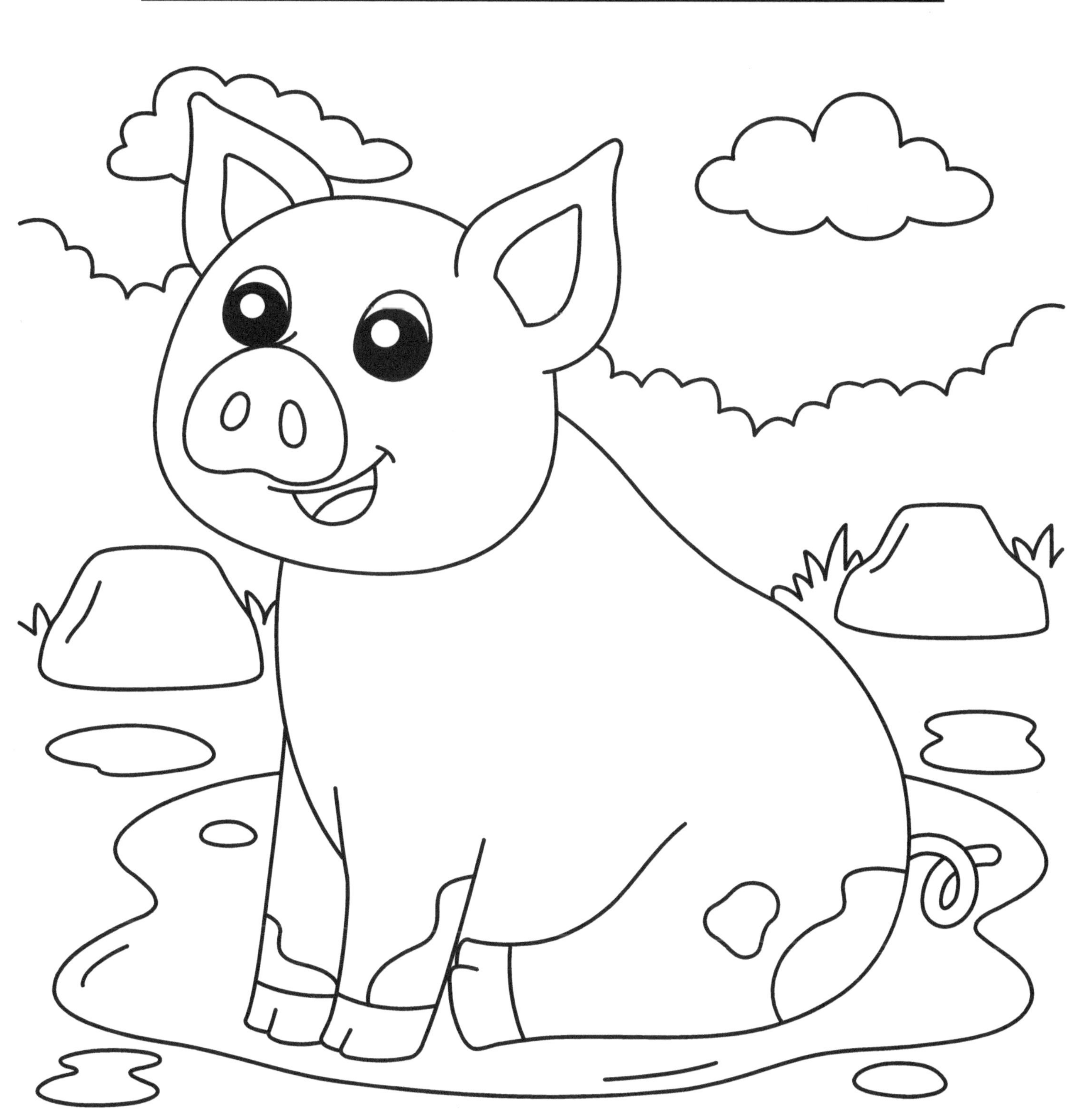

I AM STRONG LIKE A:

____

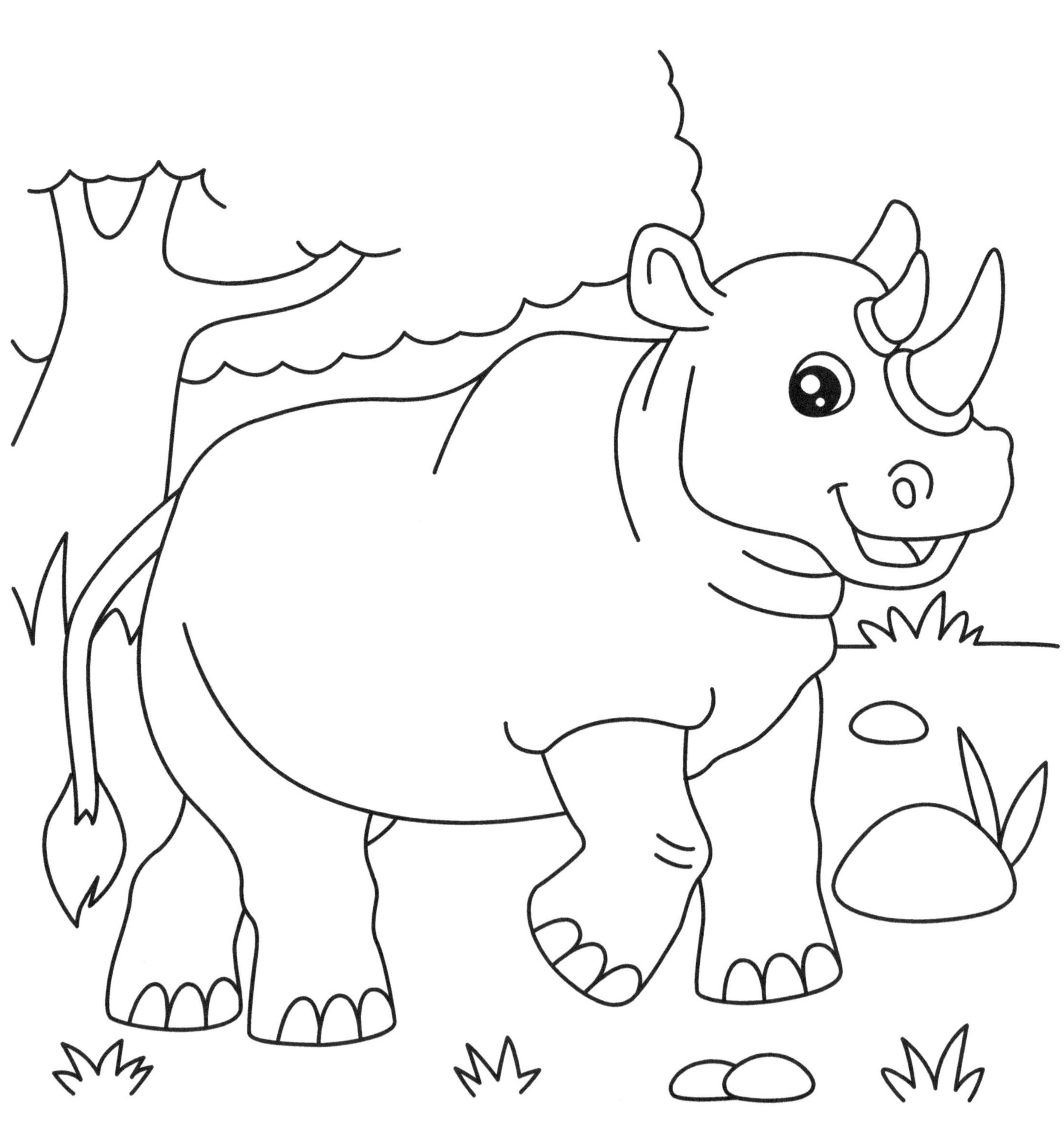

I AM A LEADER LIKE A:

____

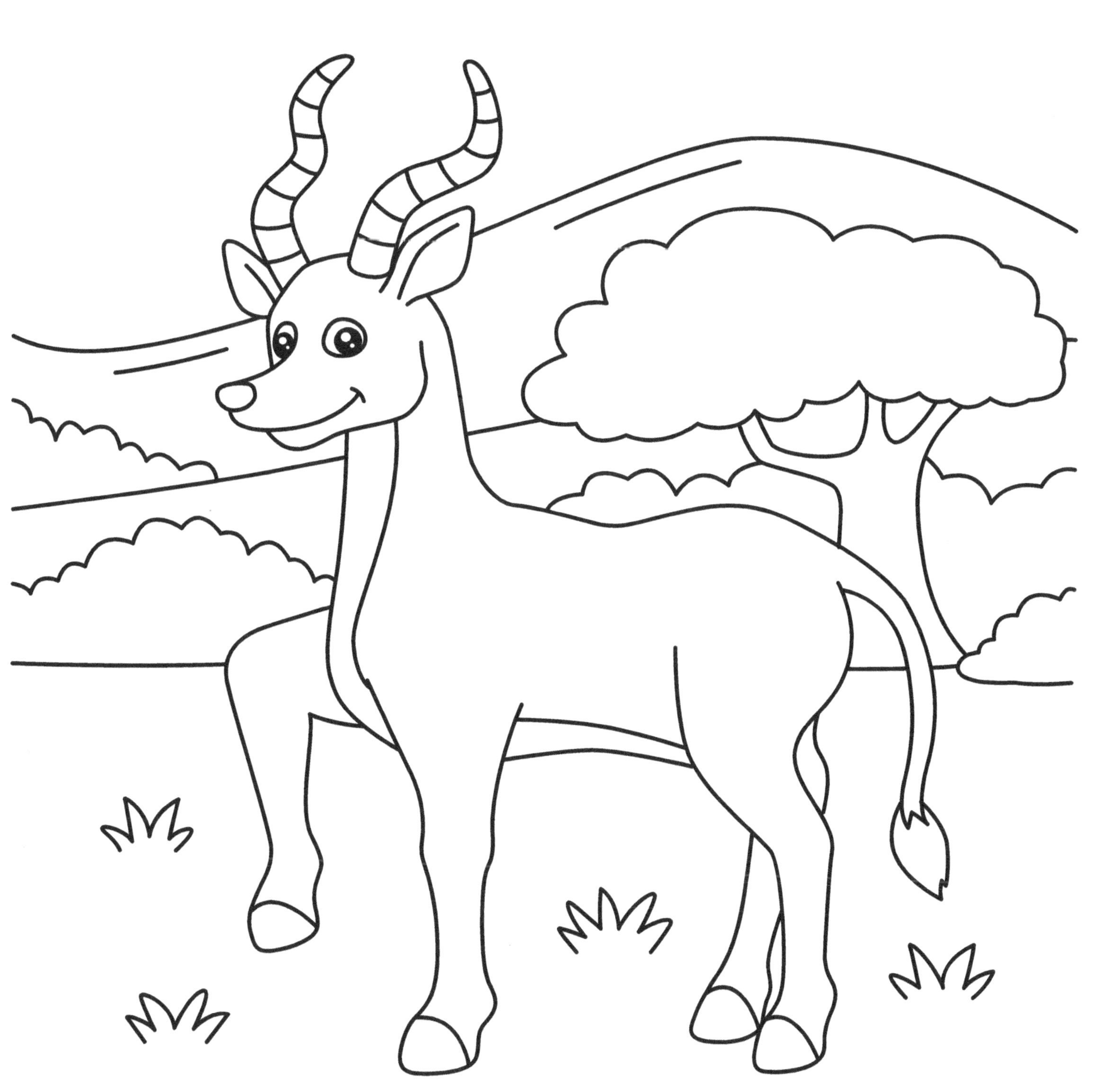

I AM KIND LIKE A:

____

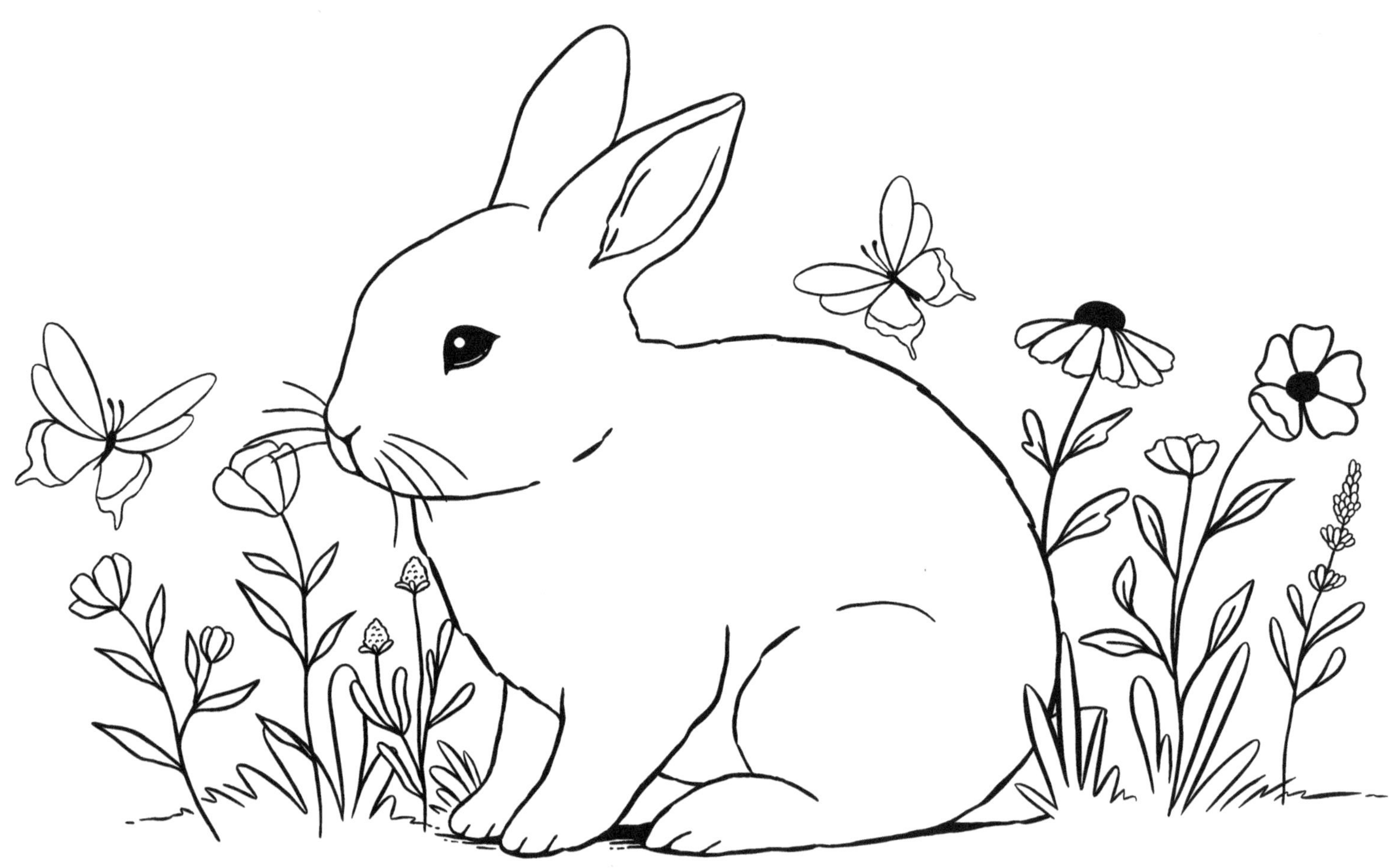

I AM FIERCE LIKE A:

____

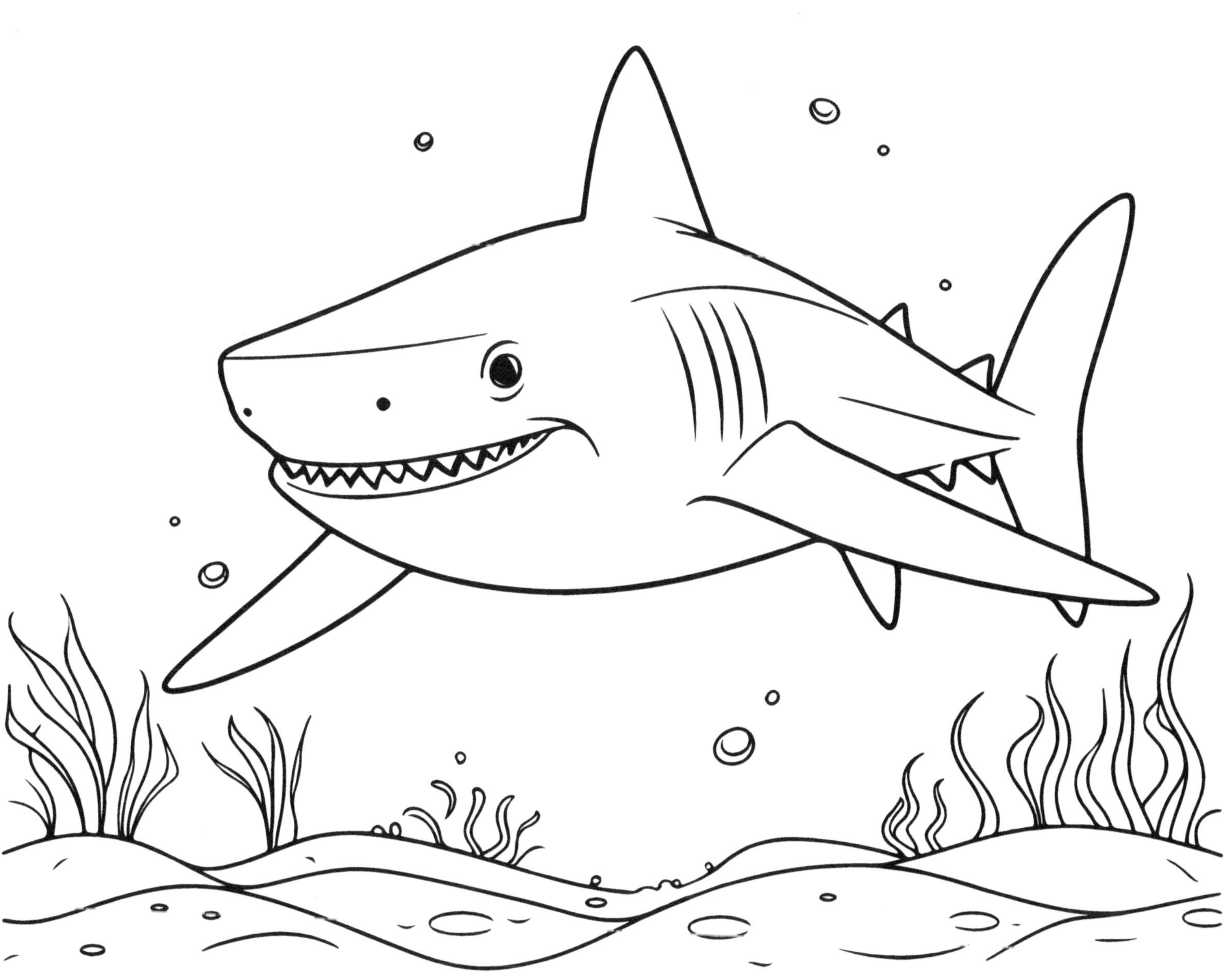

I AM POWERFUL LIKE A:

____

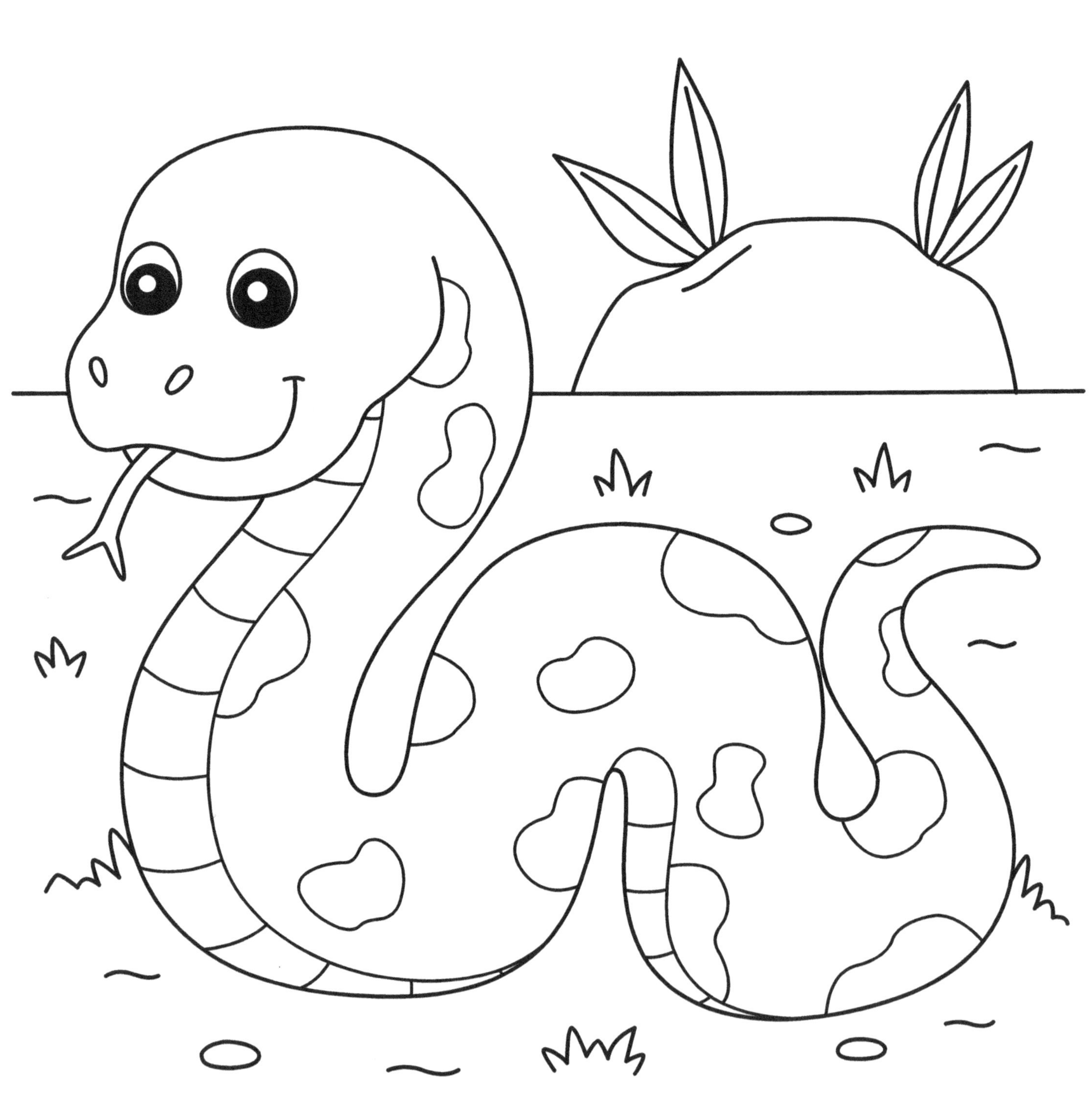

I AM CLEVER LIKE A:

____

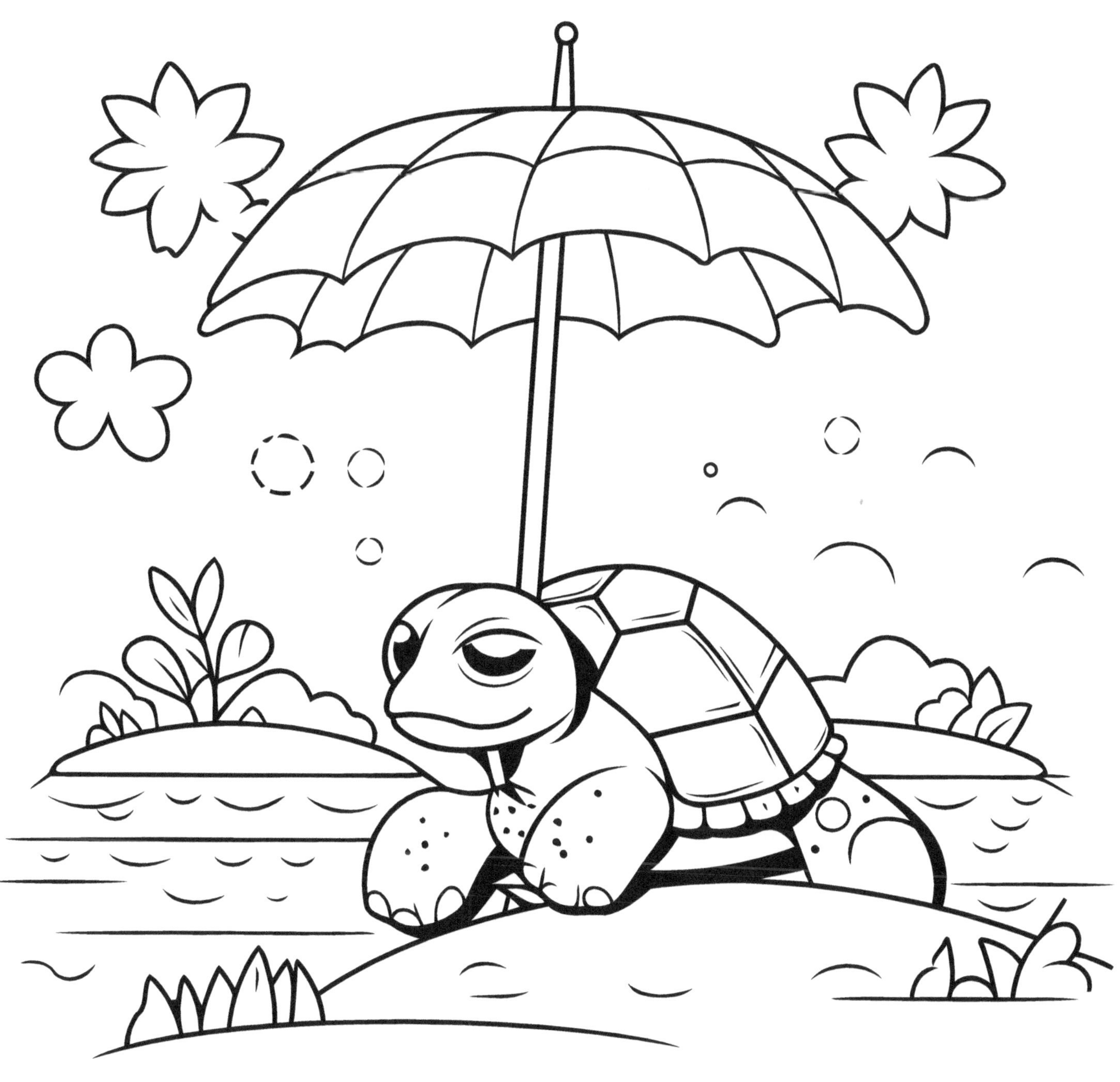

I STAND OUT LIKE A:

____

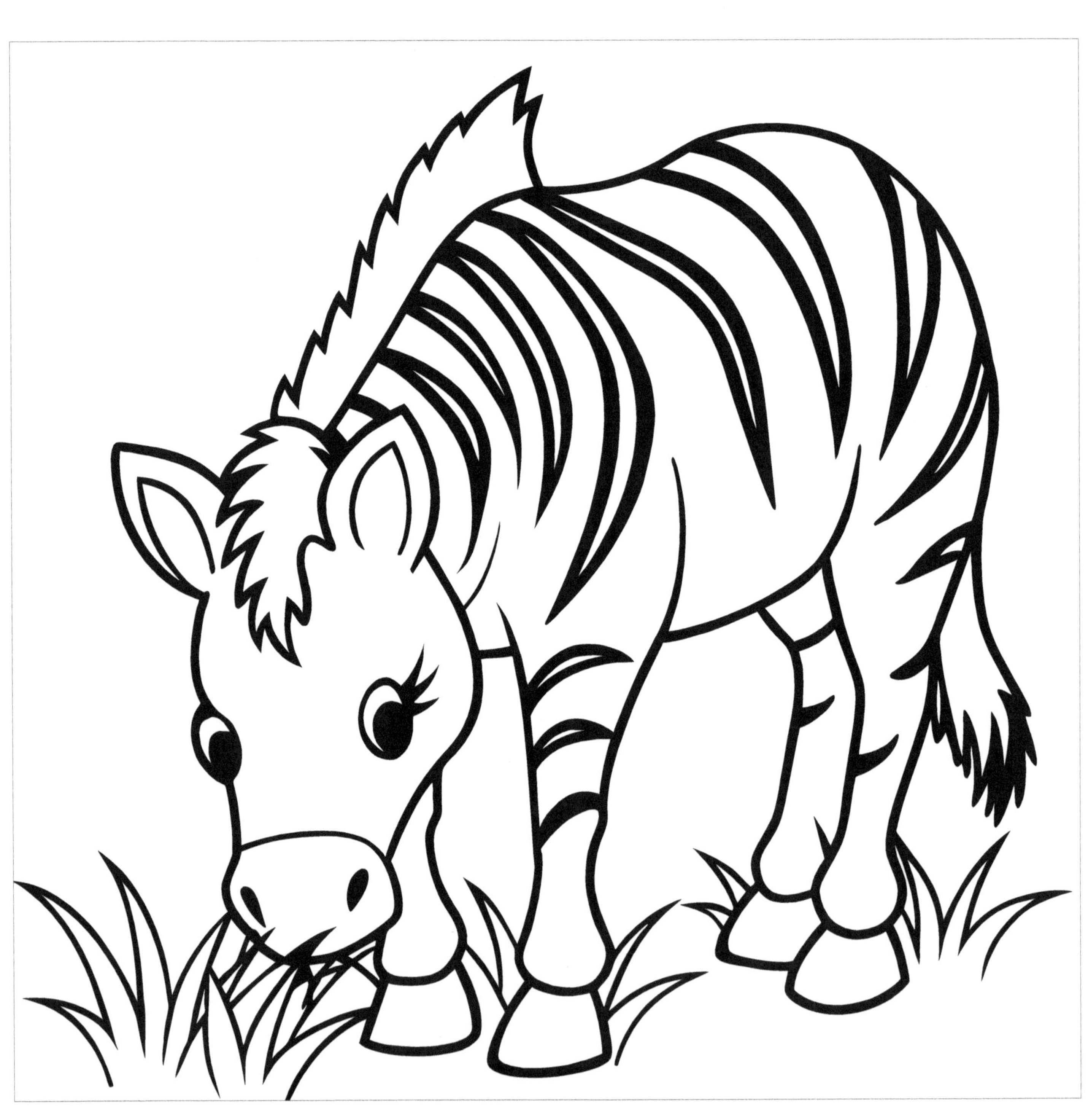

About the Creators

Elodie Romulus is the author and creator of the Kiddie Canvas series. With a background in psychology and a passion for empowering young minds, Elodie combines creativity with positive affirmation to help children build confidence, resilience, and self-love. Kiddie Canvas is her way of turning screen-free time into a fun and meaningful experience for families everywhere.

Koraun "KC" Campblin is the inspiration and narrator/editor behind Kiddie Canvas. As the "kid CEO", Koraun helps choose affirmations and bring fresh ideas to each edition. His creativity, imagination, and positive spirit remind kids that their voices matter and that coloring can be both fun and empowering.

Thank you for coloring with **Kiddie Canvas!**

We hope each page reminded you that you are kind, strong, and full of creativity.
Keep believing in yourself and spreading positivity everywhere you go!

Share your masterpiece with us:
@kiddiecanvas_bykc